THE CREDIT GAME

*A Young Adults Guide
to Successfully Building
and Understanding Credit*

By
Kyjione Lee Jack

KEYDMAN.PUBLISHING

The Credit Game
A Young Adults Guide to Successfully Building and Understanding Credit
Copyright © 2008 Kyjione Lee Jack
Keydman Publishing

This publication is designed to provide accurate and authoritative information in regard to the subject matter covered. It is sold with the understanding that neither the author nor the publisher is engaged in rendering financial, accounting, legal, or other professional services by publishing this book. If financial advice or other expert assistance is needed, the service of a competent professional should be sought. The author and publisher specifically disclaim any liability, loss or risk resulting from the use or application of the information contained in this book.

For more information please contact:
Keydman Publishing
P.O. Box 1163
Moreno Valley, CA 92556

kyjionejack@yahoo.com

Book design by
Arbor Books, Inc.
19 Spear Road, Suite 301
Ramsey, NJ 07446

Printed in the United States of America

Kyjione Lee Jack
The Credit Game
A Young Adults Guide to Successfully Building and Understanding Credit

1. Author 2. Title 3. Personal Finance

Library of Congress Control Number: 2007903907
ISBN 10: 0-9796893-0-9
ISBN 13: 978-0-9796893-0-7

Special Thanks

The author would like to thank everyone who assisted in this literary process and supported this venture.

First and foremost a great big thank you to Arbor Books, Inc. Joel Hochman, Larry Leichman and Staff

WESCOM C.U., SW Management, Cheryl Lynn Productions, and to all of those individuals who have influenced him.

And thank you to the readers of this Guidebook.

To our men and women in uniform
Thank you.

*This book is dedicated to the young men and women
in the armed services, who through defending our
country's freedom, deserve more than a
Trial & Error credit experience.*

*And to Mom thank you for inspiring
me to write this book*

—Words In living life

The greatest gift that man has received from his creator is the gift of giving. No matter how great the gesture or how small the intent, but rather the sincerity of love.

This is the true measurement of humanity.

—Kyjione Lee Jack

TABLE OF CONTENTS

ACKNOWLEDGMENTS

I want to thank my wonderful mother and father, Sharon & Thomas—for your love and support throughout my life. Mom I thank you for always encouraging me to let my light shine. Dad I thank you for setting an example for me of how to be hardworking and self sufficient. This book is dedicated to you both.

To my sisters, Tia and Te'ahnna—big bro. loves you. To my Uncles, Jerrold and Cherry—thank you for your love, guidance, and support. To my Aunts, Lesley and Cheryl "Got to be real"—thank you so much for your love and support. Cheryl I also thank you for the opportunity of experiencing the magic of collaborating in the studio with you—you are truly a musical Icon. To Thurlene- thank you so much for always being there to provide council, when ever I needed business advice or clarity on issues. To bones—thank you.

To the Smith family, the Gaines/Ward family, the McCrady/Henderson family, the Green family, the Wallace family, the Obligacion family, the Jamison family, the

Hamilton family—thank you. To my God families, the Bates, the Ashfords—I thank you all so much for enriching my life.

To my friends, Dante and the Carter family, Khola and the Nevels family—I thank you for being a part of my life for so many years. To Cyrian—thank you. To Channelle "angel baby"—thank you. To those of you that I may not have listed, please know that I appreciate you as well.

To my Wescom moms, Kathie & April—thank you so much for over a decade of your guidance and leadership. To Zerry—thank you for making me smile everyday that I came to work. To the CEO of the most electrifying company that I've ever had the pleasure of working for. Darren Williams—thank you.

Last but certainly not least,

I would like to especially thank a woman that has been the foundation of our family. Someone to whom we all attribute the planting of the seeds of faith that bore the fruit to our abilities. My Grandmother, Opal Lee Smith—I love you with all my heart…Thank You.

Thank you to everyone that has inspired me and has encouraged me directly or indirectly. Teaching me not just to exist, but rather to be existential in purpose.

A Message From the Author

*I*n my long tenured experience in banking, I have learned that there is a difference in being successful in life and being fulfilled. To be successful what you need is a good acumen, perseverance, and a clear business plan with a vision for the future. To be fulfilled however; what you need is passion, compassion, and courage of conviction. As you can see, one aspect of success requires a more pragmatic approach where as the other is more of an idealistic one. In business, sometimes we must choose which of the two is greatest in the achievement of our happiness. Well, the truth is.. both success and fulfillment don't have to be mutually exclusive.

After over a decade of exceeding the expectations of the credit union member owners, I finally realized what it was that made me successful in service. It was the hybridization of the two methods of pragmatism and idealism in order to be everything to everyone.

To serve with a willing heart while staying rooted in the policy and procedures that create business boundaries and structure. Thinking outside of the box while keeping a close traction to corporate fiscal responsibilities. Creating an advocating voice for the members of the credit union while retaining the admiration of my co-workers and the executive chain of command. This kept me profitable and viable in my employment and beloved among people at the same time. So, I don't believe that you must trade in your success in order to be fulfilled, or compromise your fulfillment in order to be successful in life. Although there is a difference in the definition of both, a dichotomy does not have to exist in the implementation of both in business. I believe that we must strive to achieve both, that we must fight to preserve what's real and tangible about life. That we are walking, talking, breathing, feeling, and embodying the spirit of our creator. It is possible to be in business for a very long time without compromising ethics, ideals, and philosophy. It is possible to give to someone without having to steal from someone else in order to replenish what was given out. It is possible to make money for yourself and for others at the same time. It is possible to make your dreams come true without stepping on the dreams of someone else.

Anything is possible living in the land of the free, and the home of the brave. The United States of America.

I hope that in sharing with you my philosophical views on life, I have opened a window into the many opportunities in advancing your quality of life. In advancing your financial stability when it comes to managing your credit. In moving you forward to establishing a healthy credit bureau profile. A profile that reflects responsibility, patience, temperance, and economical progression. This guidebook is a brainchild of mine birthed through the extraordinary human experience of service and hard work. All of the content of this book was inspired by the many occurences that took place in my life concerning credit.

From the many times that I myself experienced credit adversity, to the times in which I had to step in and intercede on someone else's behalf.

Whether I was helping a young man or woman navigate their first purchase of a car, or helping them establish their very first credit card. I found fulfillment in being useful to others, and I found success in challenging the status qou.

One of the greatest fulfillments that I've had in working in the financial industry is the impact on the lives of others. I can't even begin to tell you how many phone calls, letters, and even e-mails expressing thanks I've received throughout the years. I can even remember vividly every expression of thank you given to me in person as well.

Why this book? Well the many scenario's that chronicle my career has compelled me to create a stronger voice, in order to further champion the financial literacy of the youth. Our young men and women are entering college, entering marriage, and entering into military combat without a real understanding of credit. This guidebook was created to be a catalyst; building and understanding credit, so that you may now have a better frame of refference in your credit experience. Use this book in your educational progress in order to create a foundation. Use it for the other information that you will undoubtedly consume in your financial growth. The key to sustaining a successful credit experience is having a plan. As you read on in the book you'll learn that there is a difference in being informed about something, and being informed on how to do something. A very subtle difference but a huge difference none the less.

I hope that you enjoy this book, and I wish you good luck in your credit journey.

INTRODUCTION

*"give me a place to stand,
and I will move the earth"*
—Archimedes (mathematician)

In 1994, I was hired as a file clerk by the Telephone Employees Credit Union. To my credit I had worked at a law firm and a military hospital prior to this new company. However, I felt that my experience with TECU would be a life changing endeavor. I was right, working at this Credit Union allowed me to grow and to learn about financing in ways that I believe were tantamount to that of a parents guidance. So, I approached my job with the same zeal and professionalism as my previous file clerking positions. Although I wasn't dealing with indexing legal pleadings or analyzing in-patient medical charts, I was captivated by the language used in the security notes and lending agreements between the Credit Union and its members.

The Credit Union's mission statement is to *"exceed member expectations in everything we do"* This became my goal also, although this effort was first mainly directed toward impressing my boss. Well, my hard work paid off, and just after one year of successfully managing the files, index cards, and supply orders, my boss promoted me to a teller position. This new position sparked my interest in the lending process and it wasn't long before I was impressing not only my boss, but her boss as well. Eventually the growth of my success impressed the Senior VP of Member Services.

In 1996 the Telephone Employees Credit Union changed its name to WESCOM. It was in that same year that I found myself at a sales award dinner celebration, recognizing the top 25 sales and service representatives throughout the company. My name was even mentioned during the executive toast to the employees congratulating us all on our success. This was indeed an honor and privilege for me, considering the experience and long tenure of the employees that I shared this celebration with.

The next step on my journey was to become a loan officer, and to see my name printed on those security notes & agreements that I use to file when I was a clerk. I fulfilled this goal in 1997 and every since then I made a pledge that my style of service would be transparency. If a member saw me, then they saw the embodiment of service.

I embraced the credo of "people helping people"

I familiarized myself with as much information as possible and I approached every loan applied through me, as if I was applying for the loan myself. I became the member, and the member became me. In doing this I hoped to become more useful as an employee and as a human being as well. I realized during my years of serving people that every experience that I had in my personal financial life was similar to someone else's. Common things like the frustration of trying to obtain credit for the first time, to experiencing the kind of life changing circumstances that threaten your income and credit. Also, the awkwardness of trying to purchase your first car while knowing absolutely nothing about the automotive industry. These were the motivating factors that initiated my desire to share my experiences with everyone beyond my work environment. So, after many years of exceeding member expectations, I departed from the financial industry in October of 2006. I've decided to utilize my 11 ½ years in banking experience by writing this guidebook in the hope of becoming more useful in life overall. Useful in serving the community, useful in serving my country, useful in serving humanity.

One of the greatest pleasures of working in the Credit Union industry was the opportunity to positively impact people, and to truly project the value of usefulness.

WESCOM, I thank you.

CHAPTER

1

Establishing good credit is a choice

*I*n society today, there are very few scenarios that allow you to consume goods and services without the use of credit. Whether it's for the purchase of something small or large, credit has become the prevailing method of payment for the things that we consume today. Having good or bad credit plays an important role in everyone's quality of life. For example, the time may come for you to choose to purchase that new car you've always wanted or your very first home. Now, unless you've saved up a lot of money your probably going to need financing. If this is the case for you as it is for so many of us, Then what your credit profile looks like becomes very important.

In fact, your credit will determine if your approved and your credit score will determine the rate of interest that the Bank or Credit Union would finance your approval for.

Now, it's very seldom that we take the time to define the word finance, or what it means to obtain credit, or even how not having good credit affects you and permeates throughout your family. So, in discussing with you the importance of utilizing credit the right way, I hope to inform you, and break the cycle of generational trial and error using this guidebook as a didactic roadmap to success for you.

Why is having a guidebook about credit important? Well, Learning about credit is important to you the consumer because of the many technological advances for the purchasing of products today. Loans that would've taken forever years ago now are available with just a click of a button. This means that we have to be more informed about everything we purchase. Your credit can be solicited at a blink of an eye and the decision to approve you or decline you is just as fast. This can impact you negatively if the expediency of the credit process supersedes your ability to grasp the various concepts of credit moderation. You could inadvertently take on more credit than you can handle or allow yourself to become oblivious to fraud/ identity theft (someone fraudulently using your credit).

This has been one of the sole inherent problems with lending decisions. More often than not, consumers are unaware of any problems with their credit until the moment that they apply for a loan. In order to uphold the quality of life that you may want from your credit, you must first make your credit an important part of your life. Guard your information and protect yourself from any errors or omissions that could cause you harm in the future.

Credit literacy will help navigate you through the ambiguity of all lending practices in the vast credit card jungle. Purchasing items through the internet has also increased the need to be more cautious. With the current outbreak of credit fraud and identity theft, knowing how credit works will empower you to protect the credit that you've built up for yourself and maintained for so long.

One of the most important and obvious ways to protect yourself is to secure your social security number. If your credit is the door to financial opportunities, then your social security number is like the key to that door. The social security number is essential to accessing your credit and it is important not to have this number compromised. Those of you that carry your social security card in your wallet or your purse, this is a very dangerous habit.

If your wallet or purse was to become lost or stolen, your credit becomes compromised and exposed to harmful credit predators. These predators do a lot of harm to consumers because unlike credit cards that can be closed, or bank accounts that can be changed, your social security number if compromised could impede you from conducting your business with normalcy.

The average impact of identity theft is collection accounts, derogatory credit caused by fraudulent loans, unfair lending rates, and possible credit discrimination from improperly trained lending representatives. There are ways to help prevent these events from happening. One way is to notify the credit bureaus and to have them block your social from being accessed without permission from you yourself to solicit your credit report. Another way is to set up a credit watch to notify you if your credit has had increased activity or new accounts opened. What I prefer to do is to anticipate and try to limit the usage of my social security number whether for work, banking, or medical purposes by asking questions concerning its usage and reducing the possibility of a compromise.

Your social security number is used in a variety of circumstances ranging from school admission to hospital admittance. Documents such as your school transcripts reflecting your grades, medical and dental records, and even housing or apartment rental agreements record your social. There is literally a dozen ways that identity theft could take place due to these policy scenario's. So is there a form of apathy when it comes to safeguarding information, or is it simply just incompetence on the part of these various institutions that perpetuate identity theft. I would argue that both are not mutually exclusive; both have to occur for the perfect storm to exist. An apathetic environment breads incompetence when decisions have to be made to protect your interests by people other than yourself. Now I'm not casting aspersion on every institution that services you, but I am exposing the fact that all of the blame can't entirely be placed on the victim alone.

In a perfect world there wouldn't even be a need for privacy laws in order to make you feel protected. Until then, you must stay engaged in the process of taking care of your financial interests. The objective of informing you of these very real situations is not to scare you, but rather to empower you. To prepare you mentally and emotionally to sustain you in your credit journey throughout your life.

You may obtain information about Identity Theft and Fraud through these publicly published websites:

DEPARTMENT OF JUSTICE: www.usdoj.gov

FEDERAL TRADE COMMISION: www.ftc.gov

FEDERAL COMM. COMMISSION: www.fcc.gov

INTERNAL REVENUE SERVICE:
www.treas.gov/irs/ci

SOCIAL SECURITY ADMINISTRATION:
www.ssa.gov

U.S. POSTAL INSPECTION SERVICE: www.usps.gov

Another reason that learning credit is important is that the status quo currently provides people with a trial and error type of method for building credit. People think that maybe if they keep applying to various places someone will eventually give them credit. This has become the prevailing thought that has caused more harm to consumers than good. A thought that causes what is called 'inquiries'.

You see, there's a list compiled of the companies that you've solicited service from. The credit bureaus record this list as 'inquiries' and they keep track of every time your credit was processed by companies, whether an application was even approved or not. Dealerships are for instance a major example of how this is prevalent.

When shopping for a car, be mindful of the fact that a dealership is a car brokerage firm. If you want to buy a car from them, they have to negotiate lending for you. Whether they use their own internal financing or not. They negotiate with many lenders for the best deal in order to get you to say those 3 words that they love to here, "I'll Take It". Here is the rub, when you've given them authorization to run your credit there isn't an unwind of your credit checks if you decided against purchasing a car. And each credit check would appear on your credit. By the time you've realized that you've now accumulated too many inquires, it's too late.

This is what I recommend to you, if you have a general idea of what you like, research it online first. If you need a closer look its okay to go to dealerships and browse, or maybe even test drive. But don't give out your information.

Properly building your credit is somewhat like choosing who you want to date. If you ask a lot of random people out, it doesn't increase your chances of finding the right person. In fact, the only thing that you'll find is that some lenders will deceive you and cause damage to your credit, the same way that involving yourself with the wrong man or woman could damage your emotions. Now using the analogy of dating, imagine if when you met someone for the first time, they gave you a list of who they've dated or asked out before you. Would you be concerned if this person had asked out 10 to 20 people before you in less than 90 days? Well that's exactly how the financial lenders look at your credit inquiries.

The trick is to be cautious with your credit the same way that you would be cautious in your personal and professional life. Think about it? Your credit is an extension of you. How many people are you currently dating? What's the length of time and how has it been going? These same questions apply to your credit as well. How many accounts do you presently have open? What's the length of time and how well have you maintained the accounts? These are the same indicators that creditors look at when considering extending you new credit or when evaluating whether or not they would like to continue doing business with you.

Did you know that if your identity is compromised your social security number may not be approved for numerical change? That means that you could be spending the rest of your life with the same social security number addressing fraud. Wow! Did you know that the

Internal Revenue Service could actually have records of multiple identity thefts against you and not have a policy that mandates that they inform you? What? That's right, the Federal and State governments current policy does not protect your right to be informed. Ironically enough the Social Security Administrations policy is the same, but it's because of the right to privacy policy currently being observed. The status qou must change concerning these archaic policies but until then, be mindful of whenever your using your information. Technology today even allows you to be taken advantage of in the smallest of circumstances. For instance, say when your out dining at a restaurant; you decide to pay for your meal with your visa, and the waiter steals your visa number. That's right, you went out for a nice juicy steak and came back home 1 step closer to fraud.

Now I'm not saying this to scare you. However, the statistics show that management of employees vary from establishment to establishment. That means that at any time your favorite restaurant could compromise your credit by having poor supervisory over their staff. And the technology that I was referring to is a tiny gadget created to record your credit card information that is on the strip on the back of the card. When no one is looking, a waiter serving you could swipe it into the machine palmed in their hand while their walking to the back to settle your bill for you. What I would advocate to you is not to stop going out to dinner no, but rather for you to engage the management of these establishments in brief conversations. The more you know about the establishments that you frequent, the more you'll know if unscrupulous behavior is tolerated. Establishing good credit is a choice also because of your right to be informed or uninformed. No one is going to make you be informed. Knowledge is free, but the cost comes when you ask for it to be constructed and formulated into a coherent program, textbook or lectured course. You may agree or disagree with this view, but If you've seen the movie "goodwill hunting" then you know what I'm talking about. Education doesn't just mean knowing, but rather applying what you know. If you don't make yourself productive in your own life there's no one else to blame but yourself!

Take the time to ask your Bank or Credit Union questions about credit. Compare in contrast the differences in the response of these various institutions. Ask redundant questions to different employees of the same organization. Then you could compare their responses. If their answers are close in resemblance, then you know that the institutions training programs are sufficient. If you get answers ranging from A to Z, then you may want to borrow money from somewhere else. And speaking of borrowing, try and stay away from those cash now pay later schemes. They seem okay when you first take their money, then you find out that the interest rates can range from 30% to 99% making it close to impossible to pay them off. These company's are in the business of making money. If you don't pay them back on time or if you miss payments, you may run the risk of them negatively reporting you to the credit bureaus. Once your credit report reflects this derogatory record, it affects your credit score and your future credit viability.

When I was 21 I bought a 93' Honda civic. I loved my car! The problem was I wasn't getting the check-ups that were needed. Well, I managed to damage my brake system pretty bad and it was going to cost me a fortune to fix. The credit card company's I had accounts with would not approve any emergency credit limit increases to accommodate my brake repairs. They just declined me and didn't offer an explanation other than "unfortunately your request has been declined".

I spoke to supervisors and they made me feel like I had just been dumped by my girlfriend. No emotions, no feelings, they just quoted policies. Fortunately I worked at a Credit Union. I applied through WESCOM, Not only did they approve me for the credit I needed, but the loan officer explained to me why I got declined from the other banks. Even though I worked for the company at that time, I never applied for credit because I never took the time to find out what a Credit Union truly offered. I encourage you to find out what the lending institution that you belong to can offer you.

CHAPTER
2

What is a credit report, exactly?

A credit report is a record of your credit history. It's like a resume that you would present to an employer validating your work experience, but rather this is primarily for validation of your credit worthiness. It's primary function is to chronicle your finance practices and give a lender a way to objectively decide whether or not your credit history suffices for a loan approval.

There are 3 credit bureaus; Experian, Equifax, and Trans Union. Experian being the largest of the three and the most recognizable, it's name previously was TRW which was the former name that was most commonly used.

These reporting agencies provide creditors with a criteria to use in order to determine the risk of lending to an individual. They determine whether your future debts will be paid based on the management of past and present debts.

A credit report consists of information that identifies you, your residency and where you've worked recently. Any and all public records that may have been recorded by the county courts consisting of any liens, bankruptcies, and judgments. It records all credit lines both revolving and installment, unsecured or secured, past or present, currently paid off or past due. The open and close dates of all auto loans, home loans, equity lines of credit, credit cards, retail department or electronic store cards, student loans and of course the amount of inquiries accumulated each year.

A credit report is also reflective of how many participants are assigned to each loan. Joint credit or authorized users for example would be indicated on the report. If you are a co-signer for someone, the report will also reflect the debt under your name for the loan obligation as well. A credit report will reflect good credit indefinitely. Whether there is a balance or not, the account will show that it is current and in good standing.

If you happen to have negative credit or derogatory collections then the idea of waiting 7 to 10 years for it to be deleted could be a fallacy. The reason for this claim is that interestingly enough, collection accounts have to remain dormant or inactive for this to work. So when a collection agency sells a collection account of yours to another agency, the once dormant account now experiences activity without you having been involved at all. This could continually refresh the statutes of limitations concerning the 7 year theory. My philosophical view is this; be proactive with your credit from the very start. Never assume anything, and make having great credit sexy and fun!

Is it okay to close a lot of accounts? Well, if you no longer want to use the services of a particular lender it's okay. However, you must count the cost of any changes you may make to your credit profile. Say you have 2 credit cards open with limits of $1,000 dollars on both of them. Card (A) has a zero balance and card (B) is maxed out $1,000 dollars. The card that doesn't have a balance is a wash and is evened out by the card that's maxed out. If you were to close card (A) then what you've done is increased your ratio 100%, thus affecting your credit profile. I recommend that you always keep 1 to 2 cards with a zero balance on them at all times.

Also be cognizant of your "balances compared to limits." Another point of information is to continuously build the limits on your credit cards. Even if you don't utilize the availability, you don't want a Bank to decline any future loan applications based on "insufficient comparable limits." It is important to review your credit report at least 1 time each year in order to preserve the integrity of your information. This is very important because if there are any late payments caused by you or reported in error by the lending company, it affects your Fair Isaac score or FICO for short. This scoring mechanism ranges generally from 300 to 900 and determines your credit experience. This tier system varies in the benefits to you based on what type of loan you are requesting. This system responds to your balances compared to limits, the length of time that your credit has been established, and how well you've maintained your accounts.

A 730 score and above generally provides you with the very best rates that lending institutions offer. The secret to financial success with your credit is to maintain a fico score of no less than 700 for the most reasonable credit approval rates. The averages that I would encounter the most while processing loans; more or less the majority of everyone's fico scores, seemed to range between 660 and 690. Fair, but not necessarily great. 600 to 649 would result in approvals with unreasonable or less desirable interest rates. And a score of 599 and below would result in either automatic declines or the very highest interest rates available if the institution lending guidelines accommodated it.

Now' that you know how the score affects your loan, now you must consider what's called the 'debt to income ratio' factor. What this basically asks the consumers is, does your debt exceed 6x your income? If a consumer lending analyst is evaluating the amount to approve your loan, your monthly non-commissioned income is very important in regards to this evaluation.

Generally you don't want to exceed 50% of the bright line credit ratio. If you apply for credit and you find that there are errors and omissions that caused you to be declined, you should quickly obtain a copy of your credit report to review the discrepancies yourself. You may obtain a copy of your report through either calling or writing the credit bureau directly, or retrieving it on line. If you were declined by a financial institution you are entitled to a free copy of your credit report within 90 days of the decline. Once you've notified the credit bureau of your disputes, They will check with the source of the information to confirm the validity of your claims. If after updating your report with the proper query made to the institutions you still disagree, you can submit a statement to be added to the report that states that the "consumer disagrees with the grantor". The credit bureau must give you an updated copy of your report reflecting the solvency to your claims. If you can't resolve your claim with the institution directly than definitely utilize this option. The entire process usually takes up to 30 days. Always remember that the credit bureau does not decide your credit worthiness.

A credit bureau only reports credit by collecting information by each credit grantor and storing the information in a database for the query of financial institutions, retailers, etc. The credit bureaus do not display any information about your race, ethnicity, gender, religious preference, political affiliation, or any association that would deem discriminatory in any way, shape, or form. It's job prima-facie is to report your credit history. At first sight this must be evident to every consumer and credit grantor in order to maintain the integrity and objectivity of the credit process.

The credit bureau reporting of your credit is subject to the information that your creditors report on you. Financial institutions are not infallible, because they are maintained by people who are not infallible. Always presume that the burden of maintaining good relationships with your creditor is up to you. A mailed monthly statement and access to customer service through the internet and the telephone is the extent of their obligation to consumers. Creditors will report your activity to the credit bureaus every 30 days, so it is important that you become familiar with lending policies. Someone once said that throughout your life you would meet **3 types of people.**

Someone who watches things happen, someone who wonders what happened, and someone who makes things happen.

So here's the 'who wants to be a millionaire' $1 million dollar question, which type of person are you?

Take the time to learn the credit reporting system. Be that 3rd type of individual with regards to credit.

Be that person who makes things happen!

Kyjione Lee Jack

(The following information is publicly published and is subject to future changes without notice.)

EQUIFAX: P.O. BOX 740241 Atlanta, GA 30374-0241
Report fraud: Call 1-800-525-6285
Order your credit report: 1-800-685-1111

EXPERIAN: P.O. BOX 949 ALLEN, TX 75013-0949
Report fraud: Call 1-888-397-3742
Order your credit report: 1-888-397-3742

TRANS UNION: P.O. BOX 1000 CHESTER, PA 19022
Report fraud: Call 1-800-680-7289 and write to the Fraud Victim Assistance Division:
P.O. Box 6790 Fullerton, Ca 92634
Order your credit report: 1-800-916-8800

WWW.ANNUALCREDITREPORT.COM

WWW.MYFICO.COM

To remove your name from mail and phone lists write to:

Direct Marketing Association
Mail Preference Association
P.O. Box 9008
Farmindale, NY 11735

Telephone Preference Service
P.O. Box 9014
Farmingdale, NY 11735

CHAPTER

3

What are the different types of credit?

There are 2 types of credit, **Unsecured** and **Secured**.

SECURED	UNSECURED

LINE OF CREDIT
CREDIT CARD
AUTO LOAN
RV LOAN
BOAT LOAN
HOME LOAN
HOME EQUITY

PERSONAL LINE OF CREDIT
PERSONAL LOAN
CREDIT CARD

*T*o have <u>unsecured</u> credit means that a Bank, Credit Union, or an individual is extending you their money to use without collateral. To have <u>secured</u> credit means that a Bank, Credit Union, or an individual is extending you their money to use but with a collateralized stipulation. Collateral meaning that there is security given as a pledge for the repayment of the loan.

The 1st option of **unsecured** credit is a **Credit Card.** These are variable rate cards that have a revolving credit line which are open ended meaning that you can continually borrow what you've paid back. The variable aspect of this type of lending means that the rate of interest is based on the prime rate + a profit percentage margin that is stipulated by each lending institution.

The 2nd option of unsecured credit is a **Personal Line of Credit.** this is an open ended revolving line just like a credit card, except for you don't get a card. This loan can only be accessed directly through your bank or online. The benefit of this loan is that if it's connected to your bank account, then you may be offered overdraft protection for your checking account.

The 3rd option of **unsecured** credit is a **Personal Loan.** This is a closed ended loan meaning it's in the form of an installment. These loans are usually fixed in interest and is directly dispersed to you in one lump sum without a form of card to access the money; you continually make your payments to this loan until the balance is paid off completely. You can't re-borrow the funds.

The difference between the <u>unsecured</u> version and the <u>secured</u> version of the credit card and line of credit, is whether or not you're using your own money or borrowing the banks money. However, interest rates may vary also, depending on the institution that is extending you the credit. These versions are not to be confused with a <u>Visa Debit Card</u>. A check card does not give you credit! It is a card to access the funds from your checking account only. Credit can also be extended to you through a retail store. For example; clothing, home décor furnishings, electronics, and jewelry stores, in which you finance the purchasing of their products. The second type of credit is **secured** credit or collateralized loans. These are loans that are secured by either money or a certificate of ownership or in the case of home ownership, a deed of trust. These certificates (pink slip/deed of trust) are secured in a lien against your home or car until the debt borrowed for your purchase is paid in full.

Home loans are the most commonly recognized forms of secured loan. In Fact, ownership of a home or property should be your goal to truly solidify yourself in terms of having good credit and financial wealth. What is a home loan? Home loans are usually 15 to 30 year term loans that have a fixed or adjustable, or both fixed to an adjustable interest rate that is determined by the market prime rate. Auto loans are another form of secured loan. They are usually solicited for amounts ranging between $1,000 to $60,000 dollars. Auto loan financing terms generally range from 12 months to 72 months. Financing an auto loan works almost similar to that of a home loan.

The rates for auto loans are fixed. However, home loans are available with both options of fixed or adjustable rates with many other varying options as well. Auto loans, RV loans, and Boat loans all deal with state registration so there aren't any physical titles produced. Until the lien is been released by the financial institution, these titles are considered paperless. And did you know that you can refinance your car and withdraw the equity? Equity is what drives the market of any collateralized lending scenario.

That's why Real Estate is one of the most economically stable forms of business in the world today. Homes appreciate in value as opposed to automobiles. Every automobile depreciates in value after its been manufactured and leaves a dealer lot. The way that you calculate this value is by utilizing a free service called 'Kelly Blue Book'.

There are other types of appraisal systems in the automotive industry as well, but they're usually market driven by supply and demand, Auto Traders, Auctions, Fleet Organizations, and depreciation models creating the median standard. So, unless you are purchasing an old and very authentic classic car from Barrett-Jackson Auctions, you can expect your car to lose its value and not gain in value.

Transportation is a huge industry and should be respected as such. What I mean by this is that you should research how automobiles are designed, manufactured and distributed. Research the difference and importance of MSRP in relation to the Invoice of a vehicle. The more you know about the process that's involved in vehicle purchasing, the more empowered you are to make sure that you get a good deal in your purchase.

When looking at a vehicle be sure to research the price first. If you've decided on a vehicle and your purchase is through a dealership then you can take the vehicle off of the lot under what's called an optional sales contract. This means that they solicit your credit and they give you 5 to 7 days to find alternative financing. If you choose not to have your credit checked, then you may request a blank/unsigned purchase order leaving the vehicle with the dealer until you came back to them with a check.

There is no obligation for them to hold the car for you, so the second option is risky. However, it does allow you to change your mind because you've not signed anything yet.

A dealerships leverage in completing the sale is for you to remove their vehicle from their lot. This along with your signature of agreement enforces the "no cooling off period" that protects the dealer from consumers flip flopping on their purchasing decision.

The only way to get out of the agreement from this point is if the dealer agrees to unwind the deal. This could happen as a result of their discretion to appease your business with them or to negotiate a more profitable deal for both parties involved or in the cases of fraud claimed against them. For either scenario's I suggest that you speak to your financial institution before you move forward with either of these options. This alleviates any ambiguity in terms of any requirements for financing that may be advertent or inadvertently omitted in the process.

Knowing what the differences are in both secured credit as well as unsecured credit will ensure you of a better financial experience. Most information given to young adults today is really mostly comprised of credit cards and student loans. I believe in a more holistic view of credit that encompasses every facet of lending.

A Morpheus of the Matrix view to establishing the tools necessary in order to "free your mind."

The different types of Credit Notes:

CHAPTER

4

What defines bad credit?

*B*ad credit really just means mishandled opportunity. When opportunity knocks we must carpe diem, but seize the day with fiscal responsibility as your criterion. I believe that bad credit is either a result of poor fiscal discipline, or just the lack of information available to prepare you to make better fiscal choices. If this is the case for you, don't be so hard on yourself. The fact is that no one tells us the truth about how important credit really is until its too late. It seems almost as though the industry thrives on the misadventures of consumers financially. A sort of "gotcha" mentality.

Well, the opportunity to claim your victory over the status qou is right now! The first thing that you must do is to declare that you will no longer allow any of your loan payments to get behind. If you start with this first step, than you are well on your way to preventing any derogatory credit based on insufficient payment history. What happens if I don't meet my payment obligations? Well, If you default on your payments, an auto loan for example, your car will be subject to a repossession. As where, If you default on making your credit card payments, no one is going to break into your house and confiscate your stereo or the Smallville DVD collection you purchased. But what would happen though is this.

First, the creditors would record each month that your payment is late. 30 days, 60 days, 90 days and so on. This will affect your credit score first, then it affects your monthly payments, because now the credit card company has the incentive to exercise their right to increase your interest rate without opposition. This could result in your rate doubling or even tripling!

The 2nd thing to occur is a closure of your account by grantors request. This usually results in some reaffirmation agreement to pay the existing balance that you owe them while being restricted from any further use of your credit line.

The last thing that will occur and you should avoid this at all costs, is the transference of your account to a collection agency. If this has occurred to you consistently on each and every occasion, then I strongly recommend that you really consider consumer credit counseling from one of the various nonprofit organizations available nationwide. If you were to experience a 30 day late payment don't panic. The first thing that you need to do is to determine whether this was your fault or the lenders. If it is the lenders fault due to a statement mailing error or anything like that then you want to dispute it right away. If it is indeed your fault, then you should wait 120 days or more, usually no more than 6 months of perfect payments made, then ask your lender for a **"good will"** adjustment. This is a direct appeal to your lending company for a one time offer to wipe the slate clean on your monthly payment history. Credit Card companies are competitive enough that they may grant you this act of

"good will" in order to retain your business; although this is not a guarantee. Your credit score reacts to your credit profile the same way that your heartbeat reacts to your body movements. If there is a high volume of activity with your credit, then your FICO score would go up and down making it difficult to gauge where you are for certain.

Another philosophy of mine is that managing your credit is like playing a game of Chess. Every move that you make should be pragmatic and with the intention of a specific goal in mind, and not just a random move.

Random moves in a chess match could jeopardize your game the same way that random inquiries, account closures, and late payments will jeopardize you in the credit game. The ultimate goal is to achieve a point in which the accounts that you set up for yourself reflect the same genius and temperance of that of a master chess player. This individual knows where his pieces are at all times and whether making one move strengthens his position or weakens it. This is what I hope is achieved with you in terms of managing your credit report.

Well, what if Chess is not your forte? Okay…let's try another analogy then shall we. Let's take the game of Basketball for instance. This game is comprised of a 5 person active line up; which includes 2 guards, 1 shooting forward, 1 power forward, and 1 center player. These players represent your credit and their positions represent the different types of credit that you possess. When a coach calls a play, he analyzes the court and directs his players in the motions most effective for his system of play. Just like Phil Jackson would use the triangle offense to maneuver the Los Angeles Lakers, you too should create a system that assists you in maneuvering your credit.

Again, bad credit could only mean that you've mishandled an opportunity.

So if you find yourself with bad credit, then stop and ask yourself, what type of plays have I been calling? Maybe I need to develop a play strategy just like a Basketball coach? Only you can decide what works best for you. Here's something to consider though.

What if your best credit card was Kobe Bryant? Now think about whether your 1 credit card could win an NBA championship alone. Your overall credit has to function with a collaborative effort of teamwork just like those individuals playing Basketball. As awesome of a player that Kobe is, he needs help in order to achieve the overall goal…Which is to win.

To assume that you can have one card with the highest limits, the best rate, and exclude developing any other credit is a fallacy that could soon be costly. You can't mix bad credit with good credit and hope to win a championship in the Fair Isaac Corporation of Minneapolis playoffs.

REFLECTIVE EXERCISE:

WHAT DOES THE TERM "GOOD CREDIT" MEAN TO YOU? HOW WOULD YOU DEFINE IT?

_____

_____

_____

_____

_____

_____

_____

_____

_____

_____

HAVE YOU EVER MADE IMPULSIVE DECISIONS CONCERNING CREDIT? IF SO, WHY?

_____

_____

_____

_____

_____

_____

_____

_____

_____

_____

ARE YOU HAPPY WITH THE CHOICES THAT YOU'VE MADE CONCERNING YOUR CREDIT THUS FAR?

_____

_____

_____

_____

_____

_____

_____

_____

_____

_____

CHAPTER

5

How do I get credit
if no one gives me credit?

*T*his has been the question that has perplexed everyone between the ages of 18-24 for a great deal of time now. In fact, this problem is one of the leading reasons why I decided to write this book. When I was 20, I must have applied to a dozen credit card companies in which the end result was always a decline.

"Sorry, you've been declined due to insufficient credit." How can I start my credit if no one gives me any credit! Man!! Frustrating right? Well it was frustrating for me as well. The most important decision that I made was not to give up and I encourage you not to give up as well. I was blessed with the opportunity to work for a company that provided individuals such as myself with the resources and the tools to learn and excel. It has always been my goal to be able to pay this great service forward. So may my past credit challenges become the future triumphs for you.

The first question that you must ask yourself is whether or not you have a co-signer available for a loan. The reason this is important is that the building of your credit profile is more expedient if a parent or guardian extends you their credit to get you started first. This option could sometimes work with a relative like a much older brother or sister, aunt or uncle. Their credit must be good and the length of their history needs to be extensive enough to substantiate an approval. The litmus test is subjectively based on the financial institution. I would recommend that you speak to someone at your Bank or Credit Union, and really clarify the requisites for co-signing before you make any serious prejudgments.

One thing that I would like to clarify is that a co-signer or co-maker is strictly for individuals with very little or no credit. This terminology is not meant for individuals that have credit that is derogatory. This option on average is not available by any institution as an appeasement of bad credit. However, if you are fortunate enough to have a co-signer, take advantage of this because by your parent or guardian extending you their credit profile, you 1) get a loan without having to submit proof of income and 2) you get the lowest interest rates which is a direct result of your parent or guardians hard work and credit responsibility.

What if my parent or guardian has bad credit? Or what if I just want to do it on my own? Then what you need to do first is evaluate what you will be doing in your life for the next 2 years. The reason that this is important is because it takes relatively 1 ½ to 2 years to effectively build your credit properly. The industry generally likes to see at least 2 years of credit history before they would extend you high amounts of credit. The thing that you must understand first is that no financial institution is in business to loose money, not even a not for profit institution. And what I mean by this statement is this; if you don't have a history for someone to critique your past credit experience or a job that provides you with reasonable future income, then you are asking the credit grantor to take a huge risk in lending to you.

The key is to alleviate the anxiety of risk, and here's how it's done. First you have to have a job that provides you with at least a gross income of $500/ a month for credit card applications and a income of at least $1500 a month for an auto loan application.

You must have been on your job at least the probationary period of 90 days of employment. The longer your employment history is, the better. Generally if you've worked for the same employer continuously for 3 to 12 months, institutions may extend you a secured credit card with a limit of up to $1,000 dollars. Meanwhile unsecured credit cards if considered by the lender would generally be much lower, usually starting at $250 dollars or more.

My favorite option to recommend to young adults; especially if they are full time students and are not working is, to open a Secured Line of Credit for $100 to $250 dollars. These loans are usually non credit check application loans, meaning that they're automatically approved. It's using your own money and you wouldn't have to keep it open for more than 90 days.

As a 1-2 punch, I usually recommend that you ask a parent or guardian to allow you to be an **Authorized user** on one of their credit or retail cards as well. In case you didn't know, an authorized user means that someone is extending you the use of their credit, but you are not joint in ownership. It's kind of like your parents letting you drive their car, even giving you your own key, but you are not a co-owner. This allows the parent or guardian to feel comfortable with knowing that they can reduce the credit line if necessary or even remove you without having to close the account. The benefit is that since you are on their credit line, you are exposed to a higher revolving credit limit than what any grantor would extend to you on your own.

Be cautious with this option though, because as this can boost your credit, it can also negatively effect you if your parent or guardian has negative credit or has a poor payment history on the card that you are authorized on. Be sure to have a conversation with your friends and family about credit. Never allow yourself to be taken advantage of because of a lack of information. Gathering information is important especially when in the market for buying a new car or home.

Auto loans now in the absence of a special first time buyers program are a little more complicated. Since we are now talking about loans that are considerably more money, understandably the seriousness level elevates for a lender. This is the primary reason that everyone asks for a co-signer or co-applicant for extending you credit. They want to have the assurance that if they finance your dream car, that it doesn't turn into a nightmare for them. If you are in the market to purchase a car and you don't have a co-signer then I strongly recommend if you are working, that you find out if your Credit Union has a first time buyers program that could assist you.

Generally a program like this sets parameters of lending, for example $15,000 for 60 months at 9% or 10% interest rates. If you've met their criteria for non-derogatory credit or insufficient risk score calculated (no credit file), then what better way to start your credit than with an auto loan. Using your job as your credit is an option also available at various dealerships as well. Use caution and definitely confirm that the dealer offers a scenario such as this before attempting to conduct business with them. Always take a breath before deciding and consult with someone experienced in auto purchasing that you really, really trust.

The reason that this is important is because lending institutions may vary as to what criteria they may use in granting you credit. Some Credit Unions and Banks may implement programs like a first time auto buying loan or student visa for instance, but not always. Here is another point of information; 2 credit reports with bad credit or insufficient credit does not add up to 1 good credit report.

Most lending institutions don't define for you what the differences are between co-signing and being a co-applicant. If someone is a co-signer, this means that their credit is evaluated and used in place of yours. Their debt to income ratio is evaluated solely. This is one of the reasons why even if your parent or guardian has excellent credit, if they are not working, the loan is usually declined no matter how much money you make. Co-applicant loans are joint credit loans that consist of the evaluation of both individuals' credit reports and both of their incomes. Usually the rate of approvals are based on the highest fico score of the two applicants. Any unapproved loans are usually caused by one or both applicants having insufficient credit or derogatory credit.

The last thing that I must address is the marketing or solicitation for credit to you through the mail. Credit bureaus provide lists of creditworthy consumers to various retailers, banks, charitable organizations, and companies that offer products and services involving the use of credit.

These companies would then advertise to you with the goal of winning your business with convenience. My advise to you if you are relatively new to the world of finance is to always, always read the fine print. Pre-approval and pre-selection offers may be convenient but you should always read everything before accepting or applying. If you happen to know someone that works in the arena of financing that you could have double check your offer, it is worth your time to get that persons opinion.

The reason this is important is because when you accept an offer, you are not guaranteed the rate advertised forever. Remember that there is a difference between a fixed rate installment loan and a variable rate credit card. If you're late on your payments, or charge over your limit for example, then your interest rate could change dramatically. This is true also of balance transfer promotions as well. The most important thing that must be done when accepting any offer is to read the card member agreement or security note that defines and stipulates the terms for all usages of their credit. The marketing of credit when solicited through the mail is also tempting because of the language that is used in the advertisement.

Have you ever noticed that in the section where it asks for your annual income, it asks for your annual household income. Loosely interpreted this could assume more than a spousal joint income. Household could be defined as everyone whom occupies the home that you reside in. This could encompass the incomes of your parents, siblings, cousins, and/ or everyone who may live at your residency.

Although I don't believe this to be a negative loop hole for someone who is building there credit appropriately. I do however believe that for someone who may not understand credit yet, they may abuse this loop hole and obtain a higher limit than they are ready to handle. The negative impact would of course be them charging up a high balance on their credit card, and then defaulting on their payments, causing a collection to occur. This has been prevalent among college students.

My advice is to always remember that establishing good credit is a choice. Just like establishing good health, or good relationships with your family & friends. You can never completely control the events that take place around you, but you can always choose to control your response to those events. Take the time to be well informed of every policy and procedure inherent to the lending process.

When I first started my career in banking I was still getting acclimated to the financial arena when I decided to purchase my first new car. I was pre-approved for $25,000 at my Credit Union so the only thing left to do was to find the car that I wanted, trade in my Honda and make a purchase. Well, the dealership that shall remain nameless convinced me to accept an optional sales purchase contract. According to the dealer this would allow me to take the vehicle off of their lot before they've been paid. This was not unusual, so I didn't mind considering the fact that I was coming back with a check to pay them in full anyway. The purchase agreement was rejected by the Credit Union due to the excessively inflated MSRP and also what's called "Negative Trade-In". The dealer knew this policy and didn't inform me. You see, what I didn't realize is that by them placing me in a legal loop hole that the credit union would not honor, the deal defaults to their option that was given in the contract. Their option rate was 5 % higher than the Credit Union's and I could not control this event. My response however was to first appeal to the dealership, and they refused to change the contract. So I used my spare key to retrieve my car back, and I left them their car. By removing the trade bargaining chip, it forced the dealer to finally agree to cancel the contract. If any discrepancies or unfair lending practices has occurred to you, I suggest that you visit a DMV investigations office near you.

REFLECTIVE EXERCISE:

WHAT OPTION WOULD YOU USE
TO START YOUR CREDIT PROFILE?

_____

_____

_____

_____

_____

_____

_____

_____

_____

WHAT IS A CO-APPLICANT LOAN? WHAT IS A
CO-SIGNER LOAN? HOW ARE THEY DIFFERENT?

_____

_____

_____

_____

_____

_____

_____

_____

_____

WHAT DOES THE TERM
"READ THE FINE PRINT" MEAN TO YOU?

_____

_____

_____

_____

_____

_____

_____

_____

_____

CHAPTER
6

The Blueprint: Credit Game Instructions

Currently the existing outlets to informing the general public about credit isn't as user friendly to parents and their children as it could be. Now there are various programs and websites and even seminars that feature financial speakers from time to time. These events are usually hosted by great speakers that are well versed in finance, well articulated, and well educated in their profession.

However, nothing prepares parents and college students in effectively navigating financial success better than having a blueprint. If you've tried the other credit recipes, Q & A, web casts, and Infomercial sound bites of information. Hopefully the content of these various resources has been of some use to you. If not, then I absolutely unequivocally know that this guidebook will fulfill your needs. This guidebook is the penultimate recipe for self help because of the proverbial quote "feed a man a fish and he'll eat for a day, but teach a man how to fish and he'll eat for a lifetime". The premise of this guidebook is to magnify the most important part of the self help process…**'the order of operations.'** Now that you've been informed of what credit is and how it works, the

51

next step is to establish a blueprint—how to navigate from point (A) to point (B).

Point (A) is when the Risk Score is not calculated due to having insufficient credit data available. This is the ground floor of your credit report reflecting nothing other than general information concerning your name, address, and social security number. Your credit report is a blank canvas waiting for a masterpiece to be painted onto it like a Michael Angelo mural.

Remember, starting fresh without any credit and building correctly will deter you from having to back track, and clean up past mistakes caused by youth and inexperience. So what's up with that? You mean to tell me that I can master my credit like a JEDI Knight? The answer is yes. This blueprint will ensure you that the force will definitely be strong with you. First you have to discipline yourself to being patient during the time of what I call the "2 year phantom zone". This is when your credit profile is in its building phase. The first thing that you must do is to establish a revolving credit line with a Bank or Credit Union. Preferably an unsecured credit line, but if not approved then you should immediately apply for a **secured** credit line **(See ch. 3).**

A secured line of credit will get you started but the ultimate goal is to have your credit line converted to unsecured after 90 days. If you have a full time/part time job or even temporary employment in which income could be verified, your chances for approval is great. If you're approved for an unsecured credit line or credit card right from the start, then you are already ahead in this game.

The next thing that you must do is to apply for an increase in your credit limit after another 90 days has passed (6 months total). If you were given the max that the institution is allowed to give, or if your limit is $500 or more, then don't apply for an increase at all.

What you should do next is to apply for 1 retail card from either a clothing store, electronic store, or appliance store. It must be an internal retail card that's utilized for purchasing their products only. One other option is to finance a jewelry purchase from a jewelry store. They usually automatically approve the financing of their products especially if it's during one of their Valentines Day sales. If you did decide to use the jewelry option as one of your building blocks; once the account is paid, I strongly recommend that you confirm through the credit bureaus that the account reflects a zero balance and reports as closed.

After 1 year to 1 ½ years has passed, then your ready to apply for another credit card. Don't concern yourself with the interest rate because your intention is not to use the card anyway. What you want to do is to establish the history and a rival source of credit in order to start what I call the "Credit Cha-Cha". This analogy is loosely based on the idea that if you take a step forward with someone else, then your original dance partner will be jealous and want to dance with you exclusively. When the institution sees that there is another lending company offering you the same credit limit that they're offering, then they will double your limit. Their objective in doing this is to convince you to dance with them exclusively by matching their competition move for move.

In order for this to work though you must be loyal to them only. You can't go around querying other institutions at the same time. You don't want them to think that you are a credit "Player"... The term 'don't hate the playa hate the game' does not apply in the credit world. In this world only the serious and the responsible will get the greatest rewards, and the uninformed and irresponsible pay the consequences. After 2 years you should now have 1 to 2 credit cards with limits between $500 to $1,500 or more.

You may also have 1 retail card or an Auto Loan as well. Chance favors the prepared mind. So be prepared to resist the marketing campaigns for the mass distribution of credit cards. Solicitations by mail and on college campuses will tempt you to accept new credit card offers. But It's too soon to take on any more credit! Any more credit established would be considered as too much too soon by the financial industry. They would view it as being impulsive and decline your applications. Leaving you with a lot of inquiries on your credit report that will negatively impact your Fico Score. Some may approve you, but at what cost?

So to use an analogy mentioned earlier; for the force to be strong with you like Yoda—'patient you must be'.

After you've established yourself as a responsible player in this game then it's just a matter of time before the coach extends you more playing time. What I mean by this analogy is that most lending institutions use a matrix that determines your credit worthiness by Fico Score only. You will start to get offers from your Bank or Credit Union to accept pre-approved Auto Loans and Personal Loans. The amounts approved may be small and the interest rates may be high at first, but don't throw the baby out with the bathwater. These are the paying dues stages, remember that your credit is still relatively new.

Unless your parents extend you their established credit to purchase a new car or to acquire a credit card, expect to pay some dues. After about 36 months you have now weathered the storm. You have now received the green light to shop rates and solicit other companies for better rate offers. Within this 3 year period it is okay to apply for a few increases between the 2 credit companies, but you should not have applied for any new sources of credit until this time…and here's why (see ch. 2).

When you apply for your 3rd credit card, the company will see your demonstration of self control and they will be eager to acquire your business. In fact, I'm willing to bet that they would match both your 1st and your 2nd credit card limits thus making your 3rd credit card your highest limit! Especially if you request for a balance transfer paying off one of your existing cards. Of course this theory is only predicated on the basis that your credit history is without any late payments or derogatory credit. The strategy of increasing the limits of the same 2 existing cards is to establish what's called "Comparable Limits". When the time comes to apply for a new credit card, you have now given them a reason to 'show you the money'. As long as you are working and making money, lenders will show you the money in the form of higher limits in order to keep your business. Let them be your Jerry Maguire.

If 36 months is absolutely too long for you to wait then I would recommend that you have at least 1 of your 2 existing cards reflecting a zero balance at all times. This way your fico score won't be affected negatively with any additional cards being added to your credit profile. Having said that, always remember that credit cards are not free money. Don't be tempted to bite off more than you can chew by spending more than you can pay back. After 3 years you should now have 2 to 3 credit cards with limits between $1,500 to $3,000 or more. Keep raising your limits and set a future goal of having no more than 3 credit cards open at any time. You may also have 1 to 2 retail cards, and an Auto Loan reporting as well. You don't have to include a car loan if you already have a car that's paid for and you own it. If you're attending college, I can understand the dilemma of life's choices.

Let's see…Car payment or Food?

Although having an Auto loan would give you the secured credit necessary to establish the balance of power that you need in a credit profile. I believe that if you are happy with the vehicle that you currently drive and you are saving money, then the rewards of having liquid capital far out way the temporary pleasure of rolling in a new ride.

The ultimate goal of establishing credit is to get to the promise land, and that is home ownership at the lowest rates. Currently the cost of living varies from state to state. If you live in California for instance you can expect to pay more for housing then the national average. The median average for the price of a new home is over $400 thousand. The cost of not establishing good credit affects you in the long run when you're staring at a mortgage payment coupon that is excessive. If you were to be laid off from work or just simply in a job transition, you would be at risk of loosing your home. The foreclosure rate ranging from county to county in California is a reflection of this very real scenario. By the time you reach the 5 year mark using the Blueprint plan you should have acquired at least 3 to maybe 4 credit cards. I strongly recommend being prudent in what I call the 5 alive zone. What I mean by this term is that once you've figured out how to acquire new credit, you may be tempted to abuse your judgment.

The formula for balancing your credit is really just matching what you've borrowed. If there is a balance of $1,500 on one of your cards, then make sure that the limit is at least $3,000 or more. If you have 2 cards that have balances on them, then you should have 2 cards of equal limits with no balances on them. The 5 alive zone is what I consider the bright line in which you have crossed over from well managed credit to a possible credit disaster.

Most individuals who exceed 3 to 4 credit cards do it because they are maxed out. So they need that 5th card to stay alive! They need 1 more card to advance credit from so they can pay the other credit card payments.

If you've found yourself in this position you should stop and retool your actions immediately! You could easily create a slippery slope of bad credit habits that could unwind your progress and impact your credit score. Also, by the time you've made your first home purchase you would be tempted to use your home equity to consolidate debt. This isn't a bad thing normally because people use home equity loans all the time; Some to improve their home or some for miscellaneous things. However, this is not good if you've not corrected the causation of your debt problem first. You can easily get back into debt again and this time it would be even worst, because now you'll have credit card debts and you'll have the consolidated equity debt attached to your home as well.

If you were to default on your credit then the consequences mentioned in chapter 4 would be implemented. If you were to default on your home loan or equity loan, then you've now jeopardized your shelter because the bank will evict you. By using these credit instructions as your guide, you can effectively navigate your credit with confidence.

Use this blueprint to impact the dichotomy of truth and falsehood concerning consumer credit. Learning that there is a natural order to building credit; a chronology, that will help you navigate from point (A) to (B).

The order of operations is the point (A) to (B) process that will ensure you the success in achieving this goal. Moving you forward like a conveyor belt toward the quality of life that you deserve in the financial world. Having A1 credit will also allow you to experience the best quality of life in purchasing goods and services. It ensures that employers won't discriminate in their critique of your application before they get a chance to see what you can offer their company. It impacts every aspect of your life and can be the determining factor in your success.

Be wise in your endeavors and make credit decisions knowing that life is not a demo. The decisions you make are real, with real life consequences. Unless you have a plethora of money to undue bad decisions that are made in haste, I strongly recommend that you make choices pragmatic and mathematic to facts.

Ideally, life brings circumstances that are sometimes out of your control. However, if you stay focused on your objectives and you're resilient in your dealings with life's circumstances you should be fine.

The blue print is designed to give you the beginning schematics for credit success, the same way that professors at a university would issue a syllabus in order to assist you in navigating their class course.

This text is tantamount to that of a course study that could very well be taught in schools. In fact, I encourage any and all private and public schools across the nation to invest in the education of our youth beyond the basic modern business and economics courses.

I encourage all of you to follow the blueprint to success.

INFORMATION + PLANNING = RESULTS

Here are 3 important steps to take
while building credit options.

Step #1—Define what type of consumer you are. Purchasing items based on having a need or necessity is entirely different from pleasure consumption. By defining who you are, then you can better navigate your credit.

Step #2—Know the difference between a Bank and a Credit Union.

Step #3—Write down the information that you've learned and use the blueprinted plan of action. A positive impact is the result of careful planning and consideration. If you fail to plan, then you plan to fail.

Information + Planning Notes:

CHAPTER

7

Credit Philosophy 101
"credit strategy is a life strategy"

When the day begins the sun will rise energizing you to get up and to go out into this world pursuing your dreams. A dream can be a fantasy or it can be a reality depending on how you start your day, and more importantly how you end your day. Dr. Martin Luther King, Jr. had a dream about a time when we as human beings will finally breakdown the opaque walls of Intolerance, Indifference, and Insensitivity. A time when every man, woman, and child are equal in our common goals of quality of life and quality of love. In my research of how credit affects today's consumer I realized that other than being born, living, and dying; credit is a common denominator that impacts every human being. Regardless of your race or ethnicity, age or gender, religion or principled beliefs.

Credit cares about one thing…have you been naughty or nice to your creditors? Well, a Santa analogy maybe a bit of a stretch just for the sake of being funny, but…Give me a break, I'm not Tim Allen you know. The point is this…

Be responsible and you'll be rewarded.

When building and maintaining your credit be vigilant of potential credit predators that may try and take advantage of you. Always remember that your credit profile is just as important as your college transcript or work place profile. Be mindful of the ever changing world in technology, innovation, and ingenuity. Use your financial resources responsibly and with guarded control. Listen to financial experts, political and economic pundits, but test the validity of all information you receive before taking action.

If at first you don't succeed in achieving your goal of acquiring a particular loan, dust yourself off and try again. Learn from your mistakes so that unintentionally ignorant actions don't become continuously bad habits. After about 5 years you will have created the bright line as to what your credit profile will look like in the future. If your credit profile reflects a responsible history 10 years after reading this book, then I have done my job in informing you. The purpose of this particular chapter is to further elaborate on the idea that credit is not just a thing. It's not something that you should be afraid of or something that you should be intimidated by. The sole purpose of credit is to establish your heartbeat in the financial arena. Keeping track of your profile and your score is like having your pulse checked to make sure that you are healthy and alive. 70% of your fico score is comprised of your payment history and your balances owed on your accounts. 30% represents how many accounts were recently opened, and for how long they've been opened. 100% of the responsibility is yours to bare. Be proactive and not reactive when it comes to your credit.

Credit strategy is a life strategy, because if you don't define who you are in interacting with everyday people, then how can you define how to interact with credit lenders. In defining who you are you actually do more than define what your credit would look like. You would be defining your taste in food, your taste in clothes, movies, music, and so much more. This would even develop a clear message as to what type of person you would like to be friends with, or even what type of person you'd like to date. You would be creating a positive magnetism for good people that would permeate throughout your life. I also believe that if you don't have a strong sense of self, then you could have the same type of magnetism toward negative people or people that have toxic views about life.

Now, I'm not advocating that you have to be perfect or to live your life repressed. No, What I am advocating is for you to know who you are inside and out. Who you are determines what type of retail shopper you are. Whether you shop with a budget in mind, or whether you just get your shop to you drop on! Who you are would determine if you're purchasing items that are within your financial means or spending to 'infinity and beyond' like Buzz Lightyear. The way that you can create proper equilibrium in your credit life is to be fiscally prudent while having fun!

Forest Gump said that "life is like a box of chocolates you never know what your going to get". Well, I have to say that I disagree with this statement as it applies to credit. If you don't make the right credit decisions early enough in your life, then you know exactly what you would get. In fact, life would be like a "got milk" commercial. You know what I mean? da-iry won't be able to save you from getting bad credit.

What can save you though is properly building your credit, through the proper philosophical view in maintaining good relationships with your creditors. My philosophy in a word would be "elevation". In order to elevate your credit to the next level you must elevate your mind. You have to think in terms of the 'how' instead of the 'why', the 'when" instead of the 'where', and the 'who' instead of the 'what'. And what I mean by this is the how explains the importance of having a plan, rather than why you can't accomplish your goal. The when explains the time in which taking action needs to occur in order to impact reaching your goal, rather than pondering over where you would've been in your life had you made different decisions. Let tomorrow worry about tomorrow. The who determines your faith in yourself to accomplish your goals, rather than what would happen if no one supported your goals.

If you know that there is a particular thing that is important to you, then stay focused and press forward no matter what anyone else tells you. Be the architect of your future and proverbial captain of your ship. Plant the seeds of fiscal responsibility early. The results will undoubtedly be a tremendous tree of wealth, responsibility, and progress.

You should establish a presence in society by becoming productive rather than destructive to yourself. You are deserving of all that life has to offer you regardless of where you currently may be financially. You are deserving of a better quality of credit, better quality of financial stability, a better quality of life. The one thing that has to be monitored however is your ability to handle change. You've heard of the term- the more things change, the more things stay the same? Well this can be true if you don't have the capacity to retool and adjust to life's changing circumstances.

Today the interpretation of certain laws of consumer credit may be in your favor, and tomorrow it may not be.

To be successful when it comes to adjusting yourself means that you must be willing to persevere through ambiguity and contradiction. Policies and procedures that either make a lot of sense or make no sense at all. The deprevities of financial success that you may encounter can be offset by being well informed as a consumer. Be tough, sometimes life can be really unfair in business. Whether it's dealing with the credit card companies, or dealing with student loans.

Donald Trump's show 'The Apprentice' is a great example of what could be accomplished in the world of business. Season after season you would see individuals competing for the opportunity to be the one selected to represent the Trump name. I loved watching the show because of the ingenuity that the candidates would display in their tasks. I believe that Mr. Trump always knew who he would hire in the first episode, and that it would be that particular candidates job to lose rather than to win. In that same vein, creditors know if they'll lend to you upon first sight of your credit report. So it's your loan to loose. Instead of you applying for credit with the contention that you won't possibly be approved. You should apply having the proper construction to your credit, and then approach acquiring new credit as though you were approved already.

Speaking positive into every endeavor will ensure you the focus that you need to carry out every financial action in your life. Every action that you take is a result of your decision making. Every decision that you make is a result of your thought process, which is birthed out of the words that you speak into your life daily. According to Dr. Creflo Dollar of the World Changers Ministry, there is a connection between the words that you speak and your destination in life. I believe that this is likewise with regards to how you manage your consumer loans. The potential of getting a credit card with a limit of $50,000 dollars or more and never having to use it is attainable to the average person. The potential of being approved for a vehicle loan for $60,000 dollars or more is attainable as well.

There is nothing magical about obtaining great credit. It's just a matter of having a great attitude about credit first. It's really just doing your homework and then understanding the different credit options mentioned in chapter 3. Once you understand what each option does for you then it's just a matter of applying the right ingredients to your pie, so to speak. Take notice of any changes to your credit profile that is positive, and keep a record of any credit line increases or automatically pre-approved offers solicited to you each year. This way you can effectively gauge your progress in maintaining the appropriate credit.

Be sure to stay actively engaged in doing your banking. Sometimes there are important points of information given to you through ordinary banking tips that may not have been disclosed to you otherwise. The best way to stay ahead of the curve when it comes to credit infor-mation is to engage the bank employees in brief conversations when you visit your bank. And lastly you must utilize the many forms of e-commerce that is afforded to you by the lending institutions. This is how you will stay on the cusp of information, and sharp on your skills. Play the credit game the same way that you would play a sports game, with passion. It is with passion for the future achievements of the youth that I wrote this credit guidebook. It is with passion for the freedom of our country, that our youth risks their lives on the battlefield. It's time that our youth had a handbook, a didactic roadmap to success.

PHILOSOPHY 101

Here are 2 important steps in review of life & credit strategy.

Step #1—Define what is most important in your life. Is it money, family, career, good health. Is it the glamorous life of expensive cars and movie stars, or is it the irresistible simplicity of just sharing a slice of your favorite pie with someone that you love. Having a straightforward practical way of thinking about what is most important to you, will move you forward in achieving your objectives both in life and with credit.

Step #2—Develop a routine for healthy credit living. Create a steady habit of viewing your credit the same way that you would view your body. Strive to keep your credit report tight & in shape the same way that you would keep your body. Approach your credit with the same idealism that you'd apply to your everyday life, family, and career. Strive to achieve a great Fico Score the same way that you would strive for an A grade in school or a promotion at work.

REFLECTIVE EXERCISE:

WHAT IS YOUR LIFE PHILOSOPHY?

_____

_____

_____

_____

_____

_____

_____

_____

WHAT DO YOU THINK YOUR CREDIT PROFILE WILL LOOK LIKE AFTER 10 YEARS? AND WHY?

_____

_____

_____

_____

_____

_____

_____

_____

WOULD YOU CONSIDER YOURSELF A BUDGET PERSON OR A SHOP-UNTIL-YOU-DROP PERSON? WHY OR WHY NOT?

_____

_____

_____

_____

_____

_____

_____

_____

_____

_____

A Final Note

The American Heritage Dictionary defines the term credit with multiple definitions ranging from "belief or confidence in the truth of something" to "the acknowledgement of payment by a debtor." As you can see by this example there is a plethora of uses for this word. According to the aforementioned text the word credit is attributed to the Medieval Latin word Creditum; which means "something entrusted" or loaned. Also the past participle of Credere—to believe, entrust. Using this guidebook as a roadmap, I hope that I've helped you in building credit properly and moving you forward in life. To believe & entrust in the power of credit. I hope that I've impacted all of the youth with the information needed for them to really become successfully independent.

Our Declaration of Independence states that we hold these truths to be self-evident, that all men are created equal, that they are endowed by their creator with certain unalienable rights, that among these are life, liberty, and the pursuit of happiness. I believe that your life, liberty, and pursuit of happiness starts with making informed choices. So first and foremost, I thank you for choosing this guidebook to assist you in your credit journey.

This was the first step to declaring your independence
and pursuing financial happiness.

Kyjione Lee Jack
Moreno Valley, Ca
January 2007

ABOUT THE AUTHOR

*"define yourself for yourself
or others will define you for you"*
—Kyjione Lee Jack

*K*yjione Lee Jack was born in Los Angeles, Ca in August of 1974. Raised in the Church, he was impacted with an optimism that he could be what ever he wanted to be through faith in an awesome God. His grandmother got him started by planting the seeds of Oratorical Speaking. He gradually developed and nurtured his skills by competing at Church Conventions and preparatory Academic Forensics. If you asked him what his secret was he would simply reply by saying that he was just fortunate to have been born into a family that counted the cost of progress.

Perseverance, integrity, strength, love,
faith, civility, a Man.

—Against all odds
these are the words that he chooses to define who he is.

In 1992, multi-tasking his senior year of high school, he participated in Advanced Theatre, Competitive Speaking, and Track & Field. He graduated that year with an honorary Degree of Merit as a speaker, and a no. 2 ranking in the State of California, in the long jump—Track & Field.

Currently residing in Moreno Valley, he entered the work force early, working in many different industries until arriving at WESCOM Credit Union. Attending Riverside College and Mt. San Antonio College—he would go on to achieve success in both Athletics and Academics. In 2001, he was awarded Statewide and National recognition in Parliamentary Debate & Impromptu Speaking.

*Winning multiple medals and a silver medal at the National **PHIRHOPI** competition in Jacksonville, Florida.*

After reaching the penultimate of academic success in collegiate competition, he decided to merge his financial expertise and speaking ability to become a more useful member of society. It is with love that he's written this book, and with passion for the success of our youth that there is hope that his words inspired!